ETHIOPIA:

Where Lutheran Is Spelled "Mekane Yesus"

BY WILFRED AND ELEANOR BOCKELMAN

Best Wishes and appreciation for friendship

Bill Bockelman

AUGSBURG PUBLISHING HOUSE
Minneapolis, Minnesota

Ethiopia: Where Lutheran is Spelled "Mekane Yesus"

Copyright © 1972 Augsburg Publishing House

Library of Congress Catalog Card No. 70-176474

International Standard Book No. 0-8066-1205-3

Manufactured in the United States of America

contents

foreword

The Christian faith which was established in Ethiopia as early as the fourth century did not grow in Ethiopia unmolested. Wave after Islamic wave sought to eradicate Christianity in much the same way the church was swept from the soil of North Africa. Although the sword has been laid aside long ago as a weapon of faith, the battle for men's hearts continues to be waged.

The American Lutheran Church was invited to work in the Wollo Province of northern Ethiopia where Islam was firmly entrenched. No one anticipated quick numerical results because the battle has stretched back for more than 16 centuries and even a decade is but a brief segment of time.

Wilfred and Eleanor Bockelman, who visited Ethiopia for on the spot research, seek to relate this story. They do it with openness and honesty. They try to tell a story that is bigger than the sum total of the activities of ALC missionaries who have served in Ethiopia, because it is their purpose to relate those elements which describe the growth and development of an evangelical church in Ethiopia.

The exciting "mission" story in Africa does not center in the life of the expatriate missionary, but it centers in the African witness of those people who are the body of believers in the bustling cities or quiet villages.

This book destroys some long cherished, but outdated, mission concepts. It sets forth the contemporary struggle in which churches of the west and of Africa are jointly engaged. For these reasons it is to be commended to the thoughtful student of our present day mission involvement.

Lowell L. Hesterman
Assistant to the Director
Division of World Missions
The American Lutheran Church

there are two ways
to write a book:

we chose the second way

One way to write a book is to decide on a subject and then take the necessary time to do the research to cover the subject completely. It may take a week; or it may take a month or a year.

The other way is to decide how much time you have available and then do as much as you can in that allotted time, fully aware that you are not an expert and that you have not exhausted the subject, but also confident that you have been helpful in bringing some understanding to the readers.

We chose the latter approach. We spent two weeks in Ethiopia, trying to learn as much as we could about the church and mission there. We talked to all of the missionaries of the American Lutheran Church as well as to a few missionaries of the European Lutheran mission boards. With tape recorder and note pad we interviewed people from all walks of life, from the poor and illiterate to a high ranking official in the Emperor's cabinet.

We studied carefully two of the three general areas in which ALC missionaries play a prominent role. For the most part, therefore, this book will deal with the work of the North Ethiopia Synod of The Evangelical Church—Mekane Yesus. That's the area to which most ALC missionaries are assigned. Concentrating on this church and this area is thus in keeping with our purpose: to interpret to members of the ALC that part of the work of the church in Ethiopia with which they are most closely associated through the missionaries they support.

Hopefully this book will be of interest to other Christians and to non-Christians as well, for the whole program of missions and the international inter-relations of churches and cultures is undergoing thorough rethinking these days. We will tell something about the issues facing mission boards as they rethink their own relationships to the overseas churches and lands to which they have been sending missionaries.

A word about the significance of the title of the book: In Ethiopia Lutherans don't call themselves Lutherans. The church that is in part an outgrowth of more than 100 years of work done by Lutheran missionaries from Europe and America has chosen to call itself the Evangelical Church —Mekane Yesus (pronounced Me—as in met—

kahn' nee Yay-sus). Mekane Yesus means "the place where Jesus abides."

In this book the terms will be used interchangeably. Whenever the term, Lutheran Church of Ethiopia, is used, it could just as readily be written, Evangelical Church — Mekane Yesus. In Ethiopia the members of the Mekane Yesus Church are sometimes referred to simply as Evangelicals.

Some readers may prefer not to read the book from front to back. While the book is essentially about the church in Ethiopia, that story is interrelated with the history and culture of the country. A few chapters will deal with such matters as the ancient history of Ethiopia, the Italian occupation from 1935 to 1941, and the unsuccessful attempt to depose the emperor in 1960. Many of the readers may even recall pictures of Haile Selassie going into exile, or returning in five years as the victor, and his subsequent appearances before world assemblies, but may have forgotten just how the occupation came about. One of the chapters will refresh memory on these events.

Some may share our experience of discovering that an introduction to the background of this country creates an appetite to read everything they can get their hands on. Others may find the history of Ethiopia less interesting. We won't take it amiss if they skip the chapter that deals with that history.

We hope, however, that they will consider carefully the last four chapters of the book. They

11

don't contain stories about the experiences of missionaries but they do try to provide an understanding of the complexities facing churches from two different countries, with totally different histories and cultures, as they try to work together in the one mission of our Lord—to proclaim the gospel. It is our hope that the book will also provide insight into how the reader himself can participate in this exciting venture.

Wilfred and Eleanor Bockelman

1

introduction to paradox

We had just landed in Rome for refueling on our flight from London to Ethiopia. The pilot called together the 15 passengers continuing on to Ethiopia.

"We're going to overfly Addis Ababa," he said. "They are having problems with the runway there, and our plane is too big to land. You can do one of two things: either we can take you into town here and you can stay in Rome till tomorrow night when you can fly out on another plane; or you can fly with us now to Nairobi and stay there at our expense, and we'll fly you back from there to Addis Ababa on the next day."

We all chose to fly to Nairobi.

Two things about that experience prepared us for the next two weeks when we would be studying the Lutheran Church in Ethiopia — or, as it is known there, The Evangelical Church — Mekane Yesus.

We would soon learn that "overflying" Addis

Ababa was a rather common experience in this part of the world. Two weeks later when we were to leave Ethiopia for Nairobi, we got to the airport in plenty of time, checked our baggage, went through customs, and waited for our plane to arrive. An hour after it was to have departed we were told that it had "overflown" Addis Ababa, that we would be taken into town where rooms had been reserved for us at a hotel, and that we would be flown out the next day, *or the day after that.* It was the second day that our plane finally left.

These incidents gave us an insight into some of the problems facing developing African countries trying to pull themselves into the last third of this technological century with equipment and technology more in keeping with the second or first third of the century. Modern air travel was making greater demands than the airport at Addis Ababa could handle, and so the larger planes frequently had to "overfly" until the newer, longer, and stronger runways are completed.

The experience helped us shift our mental gears from an affluent American culture that needs but express its wants and our industrial complex makes it available, to a style of life still dominated by a scarcity of virtually everything.

It was also a healthy reminder that the premium Americans place on time is not universal. We can cope with being an hour late or even a half a day, but to be a whole day late, or even two days is almost incomprehensible. The benefit you gain is that you learn to improvise, and it's exciting to find out that you are resourceful enough that you can improvise.

Landing in Nairobi instead of Addis Ababa provided an extra bonus in that in an unusual way it introduced us to one of the most interesting facets of the Lutheran Church in Ethiopia, the number of Lutheran people in high positions of government.

There is always a certain anxiety that comes from being in a strange place. Here we were, unexpectedly in Nairobi. Missionaries had planned to meet us in Addis Ababa. They, of course, would discover that our plane had not arrived, but how could we get word to them when we did come? Our comfort was that there were 15 of us in the same misery. The companionship that comes from such sharing of inconvenience made it easy for us to talk to strangers, to strike up conversation in the bus from the airport to our hotel in downtown Nairobi.

We knew that some of the passengers lived in Addis Ababa, so we asked one of them if he had ever heard of Radio Voice of the Gospel or the Mekane Yesus Church. His response gave you the kind of feeling you get when a thousand miles away from home you suddenly run into your next-door neighbor. He was the vice president of the Mekane Yesus Church. His name was Baissa Jammo. He was now a member of the Senate of Ethiopia, but formerly had been in the lower house of the Parliament where he had held a position comparable to the Speaker of the House of Representatives in our country.

His Excellency (in Ethiopia you address every high government official as Your Excellency) had just returned from Europe where he had gone for medical treatment. "I've just worked too hard," he said. "I spend all week working for the government, and then on weekends I work for my church." We were soon to learn that a number of high government officials are members of the Mekane Yesus Church. We were told that there had never been fewer than six ambassadors who were active in Mekane Yesus.

Thus our unexpected overflight of Addis Ababa introduced us to two paradoxes, both important for an understanding of the Evangelical Church — Mekane Yesus:

1. Ethiopia has one foot in the age of the feudal system and the other in the age of technology and economic development. To understand the place of the church in Ethiopia one must be aware of this paradox and the tensions it brings to everyday life.

2. Ethiopia may be the only country into which the American Lutheran Church has sent missionaries at the urging of the highest leaders in the country — in this case the emperor and the crown prince. Again, there is a paradox — a small church whose membership includes some of the most important men of the government as well as some of the most destitute share croppers.

16

2

the lutheran church in ethiopia is small ...

but you couldn't miss its influence even if you tried

The paradox continues—from the moment you arrive in Addis Ababa. Even though the Lutheran Church in Ethiopia is small—less than 150,000 members out of a total population of 22,000,000 in a country the size of France and Spain combined—you can hardly avoid its influence on you the very first day you are in the country, even if you try, or even if you have never heard of the Lutheran Church before.

For the chances are you will eat in a hotel dining room sometime on the day you arrive in the country, and when you do you will probably hear background music coming over the radio. The music will be interrupted with a news broadcast in English that will sign off with the words, "This has been brought to you by the Radio Voice of the Gospel."

Radio Voice of the Gospel—also known as RVOG, and sometimes as Station ETLF—is owned and operated by the Lutheran World Federation. RVOG is not actually an integral part of the Lutheran Church in Ethiopia, and yet the story of the church in Ethiopia would not be complete without it. Whether you are in a hotel or a bar or a restaurant or a small shop or in the town square, sooner or later you will hear a radio. And it is next to impossible to listen to a radio for any length of time without hearing Radio Voice of the Gospel.

Although located in Addis Ababa and an important tool for the spreading of the gospel in Ethiopia, RVOG broadcasts to countries all over Africa, Asia, and the Middle East. With a potential daily audience of 500,000,000, it has been described as "strategically the most important project undertaken by the Protestant church." Again the paradox — a country where the Lutheran church is small and where the work of the American Lutheran Church is less than 20 years old, has become the location for the proclamation of the gospel to the two largest continents of the world.

The primary aim of RVOG is reflected in its broadcasting motto: "Proclaiming Christ to His World." The station exists "to confront non-Christians with the living Christ as Savior and Lord, to show the relevance of the Christian message to both personal and public life in this 20th century, to assist developing countries in their efforts to educate and to strengthen the evangelistic outreach of churches in the target areas."

The programing meets the needs of the whole man, his cultural, educational, and social needs as well as his spiritual needs. Thirty percent of the programs are directly "spiritual," including Bible studies, sermons, hymns and inspirational messages, while 70 percent of the programs are "secular," including hygiene, health, news broadcasts, and cultural programs such as music and lectures. Both kinds of programs are actually a part of the mission of the church.

Not only do the hygiene and health programs serve to improve the general well-being of the listeners, but they create a favorable impression of the church bringing them these messages, so that the people are willing to listen to the gospel when it is proclaimed over the station.

RVOG is on the air 26 hours a day, a feat that is possible in a 24-hour day because the station has two short wave transmitters broadcasting at the same time to all parts of Africa and Asia. A third transmitter, of medium wave, reaches the regions around Addis Ababa. Since more than one transmitter is operating at the same time, a total of more than 24 hours of broadcasting is done every day.

Programs are produced and taped in 13 studios in Africa, Asia, and the Middle East, and then flown to Addis Ababa, where they are broadcast and beamed back to the countries in which they were produced. The philosophy behind this method of programing is that the people closest to the area where programs are heard are best able to determine the needs of the people. Each studio operates independently and produces programs its staff feels would be of most use to the people in that country.

Studios are located in India, Nigeria, Iran, Lebanon, Ethiopia, Tanzania, Madagascar, Cameroun, and Ceylon. Languages used for broadcasting include Tamil, Hindi, Telugu, Sinhalese, Persian, Arabic, Amharic, Swahili, Malagasy, English, French, Fulani, Hausa, and Mandarin. Careful scheduling is necessary because of the varying time zones in all parts of the world. It may be morning in Addis Ababa when a program is being broadcast, while it is evening in China where it is being heard.

Most of these area studios have a follow-up correspondence course, particularly for the Bible studies that are produced for that area. For instance, the studio at Moshi, Tanzania, receives about 300 letters a week in reply to programs aired there.

About half of the letters received at the Iraq studio come from non-Christians and nearly two-thirds of these letters request Bibles and New Testaments. The radio, therefore, serves as an excellent evangelistic medium as well as providing a means of follow-up with correspondence Bible courses.

The main studio at Addis Ababa employs a staff of nearly 200 people from more than 25 countries. Another 150 are employed in the various area studios.

Thus RVOG is really an international project of the Lutheran World Federation. There were several reasons why Ethiopia was chosen as the location for the station. For one thing, the country has existed for centuries as a Christian nation and so was sympathetic to the cause of the gospel. This is important to insure freedom of proclamation. Adequate electric power is available, airline accommodations are good, and the climate is favorable.

The initial capital investment of two million U.S. dollars came from Lutheran churches in Germany, North America, and Scandinavia. The station is owned and operated by the Lutheran World Federation. The Coordinating Committee for Christian Broadcasting (CCCB) is affiliated with RVOG. It represents the All Africa Conference of Churches, the East Asia Christian Conference, and the Near East Council of Churches. By mutual agreement, the CCCB is entitled to use 50 percent of the shortwave broadcast time. The CCCB also contributed a long-term, interest-free loan of $250,000. The annual operating costs of about $800,000 are shared by LWF and CCCB.

RVOG enjoys an excellent reputation throughout Africa and Asia for the high quality of its programing, particularly its news coverage. No station can be 100 percent objective. It is a fact of life that the broadcasting station is located in Ethiopia, and the directors of the station are guests in Ethiopia. They recognize full well that it would not be in the best interests of the future of the station to broadcast new items that would be an attack on the country in which it is stationed. While a station like this can do many things, it can't do everything. It can't, for instance, be a prophetic voice and campaign against the land ownership system in the country in a way that would reflect on the emperor. But it can proclaim the gospel and bring helpful programs that will raise the educational, cultural, and health levels of the people as well as their spiritual level. The radio is a particularly important tool in a country where 85 to 93 percent of the people are illiterate.

A church that ministers to the whole person easily recognizes that in a country like Ethiopia one of its main tasks is teaching people to read and write, not only so they can read the Bible but also so they can cope with the problems of everyday life. One of the great contributions of the Mekane Yesus Church is the operation of more than a thousand literacy schools in twelve provinces in Ethiopia. Through an organization known as Yemissrach Dimts operated jointly by the Mekane Yesus Church, its five synods, and the Presbyterian church, an estimated 160,000 people have been taught to read and write. (Yemissrach Dimts is Amharic for "Voice of Good News.")

In areas where schools are started there is often a resistance for as long as four years and then it becomes a mass movement. Resistance usually comes from the land owners. They fear that if their tenants can read or write, they will be less obedient and more demanding in wanting land reform.

The director of the literacy program described an incident that points up the problem of people who cannot read. In a certain town a group of people had banded together and purchased some land. The landowner had given them official-looking papers and told them these were receipts to indicate that they had paid for the land. A year later he came to reclaim the land. When the people took the claim to court and argued that they had paid for it and had receipts to prove it, they discovered that the papers were not receipts at all. They had been swindled. Had there been anyone in the village who could read, this probably would not have happened.

The church is particularly interested in teaching people to read so that books can be used as tools to nurture the faith. Since the church is growing so rapidly and there is a shortage of pastors, literature would be an excellent means to help teach the people.

Not only does Yemissrach Dimts teach people how to read; it also produces literature for those who can read. Thus far 110 different titles have been published in the fields of Christian, educational, and cultural literature. More than 100,000 books are distributed every year.

Yemissrach Dimts also operates the radio

studio which produces daily radio programs in the Amharic language for RVOG for transmission in Ethiopia, including devotional and religious programs, and various kinds of educational, informational, and cultural programs.

Radio Voice of the Gospel and Yemissrach Dimts are illustrations of some exciting ways in which the Lutheran Church in Ethiopia is making its contribution to a developing country that is also one of the oldest countries in Africa. Before learning more about the work of the Lutheran Church there, we should get better acquainted with the country itself.

3

ethiopia—

as old as solomon

It is impossible to be in Addis Ababa for half an hour and not be impressed with the contrast between the old and the new. Driving into town from the airport we were taken past Africa Hall, the headquarters for the Organization of African Unity and the adjacent regional office of the United Nations. Not far away is the new Hilton Hotel.

The contemporary architecture of these buildings, as well as the new government buildings—particularly the post office—and the gleaming white marble of the municipal building and the Duke of Harrar Hospital (which we learned later has never been used, although completed for several years) all reinforced what we had heard so many times before, "Africa is the continent of tomorrow."

But before we arrived at our hotel we passed

25

a flock of sheep being led through a main street in downtown Addis Ababa. Later in the week when we went out into the country we saw farmers plowing with oxen and threshing in a way I had first read about in the Bible: oxen treading out the grain and farmers throwing it up in the air to have the wind blow the chaff away.

No sooner had we stopped at the hotel when teen-aged boys descended on us trying to sell us post cards and prints of the Queen of Sheba, a constant reminder that Ethiopia is an old country that goes all the way back to Solomon.

Legend has it that the Queen of Sheba in the ancient Ethiopian city of Axum heard of Solomon's wisdom and set out to visit him. Overcome by her beauty, Solomon assured her that because of her royal blood he would not take advantage of her and add her to his already legendary thousand wives if she promised not to take anything that belonged to him.

The legend continues that at a sumptuous banquet he arranged for her to eat highly spiced foods. When she woke up during the night to quench her thirst with a glass of water, Solomon claimed she had broken her promise and he was entitled to have her. A son was born to them and he became Menelik I, the first ruler of the Ethiopian kingdom.

Historians agree that there is no factual basis for the details of this legend, even though a Queen of Sheba did visit Solomon. Nevertheless the legend, which was universally accepted for many centuries, played an important part in the development of Ethiopian national sentiment.

Students who have studied the records believe that Ethiopia's history goes back even further than Solomon. Ethiopia's earliest people are believed to have been descendants of Ham, the son of Noah. Ham's son was Cush, father of Aithiops, whose son, Axumawi, is said to have founded the holy city of Axum, the ancient capital of Ethiopia. Amharic, the official language of Ethiopia today is related to Hebrew and Arabic and is believed to be of Jewish origin.

The Jewish and Christian religions have played prominent roles throughout the country's history. One scholar says that the "Solomonic myth" was introduced when the Axumite empire began to decline and "more cement was needed to patch up the cracking wall of unity." Various tribes and religions have joined forces from time to time to fight a common enemy. Christianity came to Ethiopia in the middle of the 4th century. It took its greatest hold in the Tigrean and Amhara tribes in the north. These tribes, proud of their Semitic heritage, have more or less dominated the history of the country.

Another major tribe, the Gallas, were a strong non-Christian tribe that attacked from the west and held sway over the country from time to time. The Muslims were constantly attacking from the east. The Tigreans and the Amharas were caught in the squeeze. Their Christianity was too well entrenched to allow them to make common cause with the Muslims, so they looked upon the paganism of the Gallas as the lesser of two evils.

The 11th, 12th, and 13th centuries were golden years in the history of Ethiopia, although there was no strongly centralized government that had the full support of all the tribes. The capital was seldom located in the same place for any length of time. Each ruler went from one corner of the country to another with a royal court as large as a fair-sized town. Aksum and Gondar were two major capital cities before the seat of government was finally moved to Addis Ababa in 1887.

In the 16th century, the Muslim leader, Ahmad Gran, at the head of a strong force and equipped with Ottoman Turk firearms, overran Ethiopia with massacre and widespread destruction. The country was ravaged from end to end. Churches were destroyed, priests were murdered wholesale, and most of the population forced at the point of the sword, to renounce their Christian faith.

The Muslims were finally overthrown with the help of the Portuguese, but much to the chagrin of the Ethiopians, the Portuguese tried to convert the people to Roman Catholicism, even to the extent of using force and bloodshed. Emperor Susenyos became a convert to Catholicism, much to the horror and disunity of the people. Susenyos finally gave up his throne in favor of his son, Fasil, who quickly sent the trouble-making Portuguese Jesuits out of the country and again made the Ethiopian Orthodox Church the official church of Ethiopia.

During the 17th, 18th, and 19th centuries the empire regained some of its old splendor. Three prominent emperors were mostly responsible for progress during this time—Tewodros II, Yohannes IV, and Menelik II. It was Emperor Menelik II, ruler from 1865 in the province of Shoa and from 1889 to 1913 as emperor of all Ethiopia, who opened the door to the future of his country.

The first country to walk through that open door brought along a problem that almost resulted in the downfall of Ethiopia nearly 50 years later. For the open door policy of Menelik II resulted in negotiations with Italy over relationships with Eritrea, which became one of the factors that led to the Italian occupation of Ethiopia in 1935.

Italian involvement in East Africa goes back to 1869, when a shipping firm from Genoa purchased a strip of land at the port of Assab at the bottom tip of the Red Sea. At that time the Italian government did not assert its sovereignty there for it was preoccupied with domestic affairs. The Italian public did not seem prepared to accept the expense of developing a colony on the Red Sea. (See map, page 61.)

In 1882 control of Assab was transferred from the Genoa shipping firm to the Italian government. In 1885 Italy sent troops to occupy the Turkish port of Massawa, farther north on the Red Sea. On January 1, 1890, Italy united these

29

two points and the land between them and designated the area as the Italian colony of Eritrea. Having thus established themselves in Africa, the Italians immediately looked to the south for further colonization, and this brought them in direct contact with Ethiopia.

The Ethiopians resented the Italian occupation of this strip of land along the Red Sea and protested the occupation of Massawa. Emperor Yohannis claimed the port as his, or at least his right to free trading privileges. Ras Aloula (Ras is an Ethiopian title comparable to our "governor"), the leader of the Tigre Province of northern Ethiopia and an ally of Emperor Yohannis, ordered the Italians to withdraw. When they refused, Aloula attacked with a force that outnumbered the Italian troups 20 to 1. The Italian force of 500 men was almost annihilated.

When Yohannis died in 1889 and Menelik II proclaimed himself emperor and started his open door policy, the Italians were eager to walk in. Menelik II was not as fearful of the Italians as his predecessor or the chiefs of the northern provinces had been. His agenda centered around two political goals: to break down regional loyalties of the existing feudal system, thus unifying princes and people behind the centralized government of the emperor, and to gain international recognition for Ethiopia as an independent state.

During his rise to power, while still the king of Shoa, Menelik had even accepted arms from the Italians and had occasionally tried to mediate between Emperor Yohannis and the Italians. As a result of this, the Italians concluded a treaty with Menelik in which he recognized not only Italy's occupation of Massawa but also her right to a large portion of the highlands inland, including the town of Asmara.

The treaty, known as the Treaty of Uccialli, was written in both Amharic and Italian. Article 17 of that treaty came to be a key issue. According to the Italian translation it read that Ethiopia *"consents to make use* of the Italian Government in dealing with other powers." According to the Amharic translation it reads that Ethiopia *"may make use* of the Italian Government in dealing with other powers."

The Italian Prime Minister used Article 17 as the basis for formally proclaiming Ethiopia a protectorate of Italy. Italy's claim to a dominant position in Ethiopia was accepted by the British. In 1891 British Italian agreements designated almost all of Ethiopia, including the western Ethiopian highlands, as an Italian sphere of influence.

When Menelik discovered how Italy was using Article 17, he protested at once to Rome. One advantage to Menelik was that this danger of Italian encroachment served his purpose of centralization. The need for unity to face an outside danger gave him the opportunity to force the chiefs of the provinces to subordinate themselves to his political direction.

The Italians began to move inland. They had decided on war. George W. Baer writes in his

The Coming of the Italian-Ethiopian War: "In their line of advance lay the holy city of Aksum, the spiritual center of Ethiopian civilization. The defense of this territory gave Menelik's campaign a crusading quality, and he mustered men in the name of Ethiopian nationalism. Italian hopes for Ethiopian disunity were not fulfilled—all the great chiefs fell into line behind the emperor . . . On March 1, 1896, the Italian army, prodded by the home government in an incautious advance, met Menelik's troops at Aduwa, the old capital of Tigre. There an Ethiopian army of some 100,000 men routed the Italian force of 17,700 metropolitan and colonial troops, 10,596 of whom were Europeans. Italian casualties amounted to some 6,000 men killed, 2,000 wounded, and 2,000 taken prisoner. For the Ethiopians, Aduwa was the greatest military victory in their history. It put Ethiopia on the map of the world. For the Italians, Aduwa was the greatest military defeat incurred by any European nation at the hands of Africans in all of the 19th century."

Thus was laid the basis for an international grudge that 40 years later Italy would use to spur its people to avenge this humiliating defeat. Then they would be dealing with an emperor in Ethiopia of even greater stature than Menelik II. That man would be Haile Selassie.

Haile Selassie's father was Ras Makonnen, a cousin of Menelik II as well as his chief diplomat and soldier. Young Selassie gained a western education from a French Catholic mission and showed outstanding qualities—including ambition—very early. Menelik thought highly of him and gave him a number of responsible posts. When Menelik died he was succeeded by one of his grandsons, Yasu. Yasu's reign was a disaster. He offended the priests by embracing the Muslim faith, which, says John Gunther, "is as if the King of England should suddenly become Buddhist."

Yasu was deposed, and Haile Selassie, who at that time still went by the name Tafari Makonnen was brought forward to replace him. But he could not yet be made Emperor. The succession went to Empress Zauditu, one of Menelik's daughters, but Selassie became regent and heir to the throne. In 1928 he became King of Shoa, an important province, and in 1930, when Zauditu died, he was crowned emperor.

This was also the time that Mussolini was beginning to think that Italy should have colonies as did other European countries. Since Italy already had a foothold in Eritrea, it was only natural for him to think of going south from there, and that meant Ethiopia. Furthermore, there was that humiliating defeat of 1891 to avenge.

Haile Selassie was well aware of the Duce's plans, and so against great odds he engineered Ethiopia's membership in the League of Nations. He applied for membership in 1923 with the sponsorship of France. Mussolini realized that Ethiopia's admission to the league would be contrary to Italy's colonial interests, and he decided to oppose it. However, since it became obvious

33

that two-thirds of the league membership would approve the admission, Mussolini did not want to risk the ill will of other states and increase the enmity of Ethiopia and so he offered his endorsement. The first test case of the value of the League of Nations membership came in 1926.

In 1906 Britain, France, and Italy, without consulting Ethiopia, had concluded a tripartite treaty in which they had defined their respective interests in Ethiopia and laid a guideline for any future colonial activity. The three European governments agreed to safeguard each other's interest and, to prevent any unbridled action, decided that all military expeditions in Ethiopia had to be undertaken jointly. Unilateral intervention was ruled out.

But in 1925 Britain and Italy, without consulting either France or Ethiopia, reached an agreement that recognized exclusive Italian influence in the western part of Ethiopia. The French were angry for not having been consulted, but they raised no strong objection, hoping that the objection might come from other sources. It did come—from Haile Selassie. He took the case before the League of Nations.

Response to Ethiopia's complaint came quickly. Britain and Italy sent notes to the secretary-general of the league immediately, protesting that neither country had any aggressive designs on Ethiopia. The two countries' representatives in Addis Ababa assured Selassie of their governments' desire for friendly relations with Ethiopia.

For the Ethiopians, Selassie's appeal to the league seemed to demonstrate in a striking way how a weak state could use the international organization as protection against the greater powers.

But Mussolini had his mind set on establishing colonies and Ethiopia seemed to be the only possibility in sight. He began to build an army. All that remained was to find an incident that would justify his action before the world. The Walwal incident in December of 1934 provided him with a cause.

In the eastern part of Ethiopia near the border of Italian Somaliland is a desert where watering places are few and far between. Over this vast dry wilderness of thornbush and elephant grass Somali tribes wander with their herds of camels, goats, sheep, and long-horned cattle. During the dry season they are compelled to stay near the water holes. The wells of Walwal provide such watering holes. Boundary lines are not too carefully drawn in this area, and there is room for arguments on both sides as to who has "property rights." The Italians sent a contingent of soldiers to the area to establish it as a proper frontier post and build a fort. There was never any doubt that a clash was sure to come. It came on December 5, 1934. Who fired the first shot has never been established; each side said it was the other.

Mussolini demanded an apology, a salute to the Italian flag, recognition of Italy's legitimate rights to Walwal, punishment of the offenders, and the equivalent of $100,000 compensation.

This time Selassie was not able to get the League of Nations to back him, and this marked the turning point of the effectiveness of the League. The Italians invaded Ethiopia in 1935, and on May 5, 1936, the Emperor went into exile in England. Exactly five years later, May 5, 1941, he came back to his country.

With the exception of the unsuccessful attempted overthrow of the Emperor in 1960 (which will be described in a later chapter) there has never been any doubt of his absolute control over the affairs of the country. For many people Haile Selassie is synonymous with Ethiopia itself. In a slightly less sense he is also synonymous with the Ethiopian Orthodox Church.

4

christianity in ethiopia—

as old as the book of acts

Not only is Ethiopia one of the oldest countries on the African continent, but the Christian church in Ethiopia is also one of the oldest Christian churches in Africa. We first read of Christianity there in the eighth chapter of the book of Acts, which describes the encounter between Philip and the Ethiopian eunuch. Presumably the eunuch went back to his home in Ethiopia and spread the gospel there. Undoubtedly there were individual converts, but we know of no organized churches that came from these efforts.

In the middle of the fourth century there was a shipwreck on the Red Sea, and two lone survivors were swept ashore on the coast of Ethiopia. One of these was Frumentius, a young Greek of the Syrian Orthodox Church. He quickly won the favor of the Ethiopian empress and was made court treasurer. Through his efforts the whole imperial family and court were converted to Christianity. Frumentius was asked to go back to Syria and bring back more priests so that the gospel could be brought to other people in the country.

Instead of returning to Syria, Frumentius stopped in Alexandria on the Nile delta and put his problem to the Patriarch of the Egyptian Coptic Church. Priests were supplied and Frumentius was made Archbishop of Ethiopia. The Patriarch of Alexandria who consecrated him was the famous Athanasius, well known in early Christian history. This relationship with the Alexandrian Patriarch of the Egyptian Coptic Church and its influence in Ethiopia continued to the middle of the 20th century.

Haile Selassie ended this arrangement after his return from Exile in 1941. When the last Egyptian Abuna (roughly, archbishop or metropolitan) died, the emperor refused to accept a new one. He wanted the leadership to be Ethiopian. Delicate negotiations with the Alexandrian patriarch were necessary before he had his way. He had to tread carefully because he did not want to break too sharply with tradition. Now the emperor nominates a man (always an Ethiopian), who is suggested by the local clergy, and this nomination is then "confirmed" by the Patriarch in Alexandria. The Patriarch no longer has any actual choice. His confirmation of the emperor's nomination is a mere formality. Although many Copts bitterly resented the emperor's action, there was nothing they could do about it. Many people still speak of the church in Ethiopia as the Coptic Church, but the Ethiopians themselves are quite insistent that it be called the Ethiopian Orthodox Church.

As is so often true when a religion is a state religion, there is a large gap between the priests and the people. This is particularly the case when the religious organization gets a large part of its income from the state, as is the case in Ethiopia. The gap becomes even wider and deeper when the majority of the masses cannot read or write and are in poverty, as also is the case in Ethiopia.

It is estimated that 35 percent of all Ethiopians are members of the Ethiopian Orthodox Church. Another 35 percent are Muslims. Other church groups account for 5 percent; and 25 percent are said to be pagans. The Orthodox church has never had a program of evangelizing those outside the church or systematically nurturing the faith of its own members.

As with so many other things in Ethiopia, the Orthodox Church also is a paradox. Dr. Joseph Simonson, a pastor of the American Lutheran Church, who served as United States Ambassador to Ethiopia from 1953 to 1957, says: "The Ethiopian Orthodox Church, like many state churches elsewhere, is inclined toward laziness and unconcern both for the practical expression of the Christian faith in life and for the unbelief of those outside the church. There is the temptation toward a lack of concern both inside and outside the church. Self-satisfaction easily creeps into a church existing rather comfortably over so many centuries."

But Ambassador Simonson also expressed the conviction that the church is influential in the lives of people, even though it doesn't seem so. He tells of going to a midnight Christmas mass that lasted from 12 o'clock midnight until 8 o'clock in the morning. The actual mass itself took only about an hour and a half; the other six and a half hours were spent in chanting Psalms. The church was packed and he estimated another 8,000 gathered outside.

Until very recently the only language used in worship has been Ge'ez, an ancient tongue of the original Semitic people of Ethiopia, a language that is not understood by the common people. (The situation is similar to the use of Latin by the Catholic church in this country when few people understood it.) Not until 1934 was there an official, revised translation of the liturgy into Amharic, the official government language. More recently some of the liturgies have been translated into English. The education level of the priests has usually been quite low. One of the chief qualifications has been the ability to chant the liturgy in the Ge'ez language. Some of the priests cannot read or write themselves but must learn to chant the liturgy from memory. The priesthood is largely an inherited office, passed down from father to son without regard to ability.

On the other hand, the Orthodox church did

contribute to the educational system of the country. In fact, before government schools and mission schools became available, it provided the only educational system. It conducted "priests' schools" in various parts of the country. While these schools may have been intended largely for the perpetuation of the priesthood and left much to be desired educationally, they did make a dent in the illiteracy of the country.

One missionary in explaining the difference between the Ethiopian Orthodox Church and the Lutherans said that for the Orthodox, Christianity is not related to knowledge or faith but rather with who I am. The Orthodox Christian says simply, "I am a Christian. Christ is my savior. I have been baptized."

He has done little to think through what this means. The whole relationship of Christianity to morality is foreign to him. Some of the symbolism of Christianity is very meaningful to him. He goes to church for baptisms, weddings, and funerals. He knows that there is a vast difference between Christians and Muslims although he can't articulate intellectually what that difference is. He knows, for instance, that a Christian never eats meat that has been slaughtered by Muslims. He has a deep feeling about the binding quality of the sacrament. If a husband and wife go to communion together they feel they are bound together for life. That may be the reason they seldom go to communion together—to leave a loophole in case they might want to separate some day.

His Excellency Ato Emanuel Abraham, who is the Minister of Mines in the Emperor's cabinet, and also the president of the Mekane Yesus Church, said, "For over a thousand years we fought for our faith. It wasn't until the Italian invasion in 1890 that we fought for our country. From 700 to 1889, we fought the Muslims. Whenever there was a war, the rallying cry was to save the faith. Whatever weakness the Orthodox church may have had, it kept Christ alive in the consciousness of the people so that they were willing to fight for the faith."

The relationship of the Ethiopian Orthodox Church to the Lutheran church is also something of a paradox. On the one hand, the Emperor himself is a devout member of the Orthodox church and looks with disfavor upon any missionaries who deliberately try to get members away from the Orthodox church. On the other hand, the emperor gave his full blessing to the American Lutheran Church and encouraged it to send missionaries to Ethiopia.

It's understandable that the Ethiopian Orthodox Church should feel threatened and fear a loss of power and control over people if missionaries get too large a following. While in some places the Orthodox church is still strongly opposed to the Lutheran church, in other places there is a growing acceptance. One of the underlying principles of the Lutheran church in Ethiopia

is to help bring about renewal within the Orthodox church.

Ambassador Simonson tells of a conversation
he had with Theophilos who is now the Patriarch
of the Ethiopian Orthodox Church. The Ethiopian
church leader told Simonson, "I know our church
ought to do more mission work, but we don't
know how to do it. You'll have to help us."

5

lutheranism in ethiopia—

more than 100 years old

Although the American Lutheran Church did not send missionaries to Ethiopia until 1957, Lutheran work in that country dates back to 1866, when the Swedish Evangelical Mission began work in Eritrea, an Italian colony in the north, which has since become a part of Ethiopia. Swedish missionaries had also hoped to reach the pagan Galla tribe in the west, but only sporadic and short attempts were made. No formally constituted congregations were established within this part of Ethiopia, except for the church in Eritrea, which was founded in 1925.

Lutheran missionaries from Germany, Norway, and Denmark were active in other parts of the country but with no phenomenal success. Missionaries who were particularly gifted in the field of education caught the attention of the government and were given a free hand to develop schools. During these years there was no attempt to bring all these Lutherans together under one church run by the Ethiopians themselves.

Then came the Italian occupation under Mussolini from 1936 to 1941, and what little success there had been in 70 years seemed doomed. Evangelical Christians were persecuted. Very few had formal education. Some who had reached secondary school age and had finances were sent abroad to finish their education.

During the occupation a number of evangelical Christians left Eritrea and settled in Addis Ababa, because jobs and opportunities for further education were not very good in Eritrea. The Italians wanted to use the nationals only as very minor clerks and in demeaning and subordinate tasks.

These Evangelicals who came from Eritrea formed a congregation in Addis Ababa, which became the mother congregation of Mekane Yesus. They assumed responsibility for the Evangelical groups, which consisted of very few believers.

As has happened so often in the history of missions, when missionaries have been forced to leave the country and the struggling young church is thrown on its own it has developed more strength than either they or the missionaries felt was possible. When the Swedish missionaries returned after the defeat of the Italians they found the nucleus of a strong Lutheran church.

At the same time that the Swedish missionaries were re-establishing their work in the north, through the work of the German Hermannsburg Mission a spiritual awakening was taking place in the west. One of their missionaries acted as an overall pastor, traveling far and wide, nurturing those scattered Evangelical Christians. During the years 1946-1948 a wider spiritual awakening took place, and it resulted in the formation of congregations.

Some Orthodox priests had also joined the Evangelical movement, but the Orthodox church soon put pressure on them and accused them of leaving the faith of their fathers. Local authorities, following the requests of some Orthodox priests, used imprisonment and various kinds of persecution to try to reclaim former priests and members of the Orthodox church.

On the other hand, the Orthodox church excommunicated many who had joined the Evangelical movement and refused to baptize their children or bury their dead in sacred ground. These people, who were thus left without nurture came to the Lutherans and asked for membership in what was not yet a church. Although there were some scattered congregations there was no possibility of assimilating the new members and giving them proper instruction. For years there was only one pastor and two or three missionary families in the area. The beginnings of the church, therefore, were largely dependent upon a lay movement.

In 1948 the Norwegian Lutheran missionaries arrived and started to work in the south. Because of the good work of all of these missionaries, the Lutheran church was highly respected by the Imperial family.

In the early 1950s, the Crown Prince Asfa Wasen requested the Swedish Evangelical mission director, the Rev. P. Stjarne, to begin work in the Wollo Province, northeast of Addis Ababa.

Because Swedish Lutherans already had heavy commitments in Eritrea in northern Ethiopia and in the Wallega Province in western Ethiopia, they were unable to respond positively to the Crown Prince's request. Instead, they forwarded the invitation to the Lutheran World Federation in Geneva, who in turn forwarded it to the National Lutheran Council's office in New York, who sent it on to the National office of the American Lutheran Church in Columbus, Ohio. (This is not the present American Lutheran Church but one of the predecessor bodies, also known as the American Lutheran Church which united in 1960 with the Evangelical Lutheran Church and the United Evangelical Lutheran Church to form what we now know as The American Lutheran Church.)

This former American Lutheran Church, which until that time had been sending missionaries only to India and New Guinea had been considering larger responsibilities. The church considered three new areas—Tanzania, Iraq, and Ethiopia. In 1954 the Board of Foreign Missions of the former ALC authorized its executive secretary, Dr. Theodore P. Fricke, to go to Ethiopia and explore the possibilities of establishing a new mission there. Since at that time the ALC was already in consultation with the larger Evangelical Lutheran Church for a possible merger, Dr. Rolf

Syrdal, executive secretary of the Board of Foreign Missions of the ELC, accompanied Dr. Fricke.

Since the U. S. Ambassador to Ethiopia at the time, Dr. Joseph Simonson, had been a pastor of the American Lutheran Church, Dr. Fricke and Dr. Syrdal were guests at the residence of the ambassador. Ambassador Simonson arranged a two-day stay in Dessie as the guests of the Crown Prince. They were given a warm welcome and assured of the Crown Prince's full cooperation in getting locations in the Wollo Province. Two places were recommended: a hospital in Waldia and a mission station in Dessie, the provincial capital of Wollo. Since Wollo province has a large percentage of Muslims, the Crown Prince expressed the hope that these people might become Christians. The Emperor himself was also deeply committed to the evangelization of the Muslims.

Dr. Fricke and Dr. Syrdal also met with the representatives of other Lutheran missions in Ethiopia and they encouraged the American Lutherans to begin work in the Wollo province.

Ambassador Simonson reports that while the emperor was obviously very interested in having American Lutheran missionaries come to Ethiopia, the red tape of his government made it difficult for them to get the official permission to enter. In his last two official visits to the imperial palace before returning to the United States, Ambassador Simonson reminded the Emperor that the official papers granting permission to the American Lutheran mission had not yet come through. The Emperor seemed surprised, and when two days before his departure, Ambassador Simonson reminded him again, the Emperor —in the presence of the ambassador—called one of his cabinet ministers and personally insisted that the matter be taken care of immediately. Permission finally came on the next afternoon at four o'clock. The next morning the Simonsons left for the United States. It may be idle speculation to wonder whether American Lutherans would have gotten into Ethiopia had it not been for a sympathetic ambassador.

The Rev. Herbert G. Schaefer of Renigunta, India, was called as the "organizer and administrator" of the ALC mission in Ethiopia. Missionary Schaefer is the son of missionaries to India and had himself returned to India as a missionary after completing seminary in the United States.

Missionary Schaefer and his family arrived in Addis Ababa on September 17, 1957. Other missionaries to arrive within eight months were Rev. and Mrs. Rudy Wendel, Mr. and Mrs. William Wright, Rev. and Mrs. Thomas Damrow, and Rev. and Mrs. Lowell Hesterman. The work had hardly started when the Swedish Evangelical Mission asked the ALC Mission also to assume responsibility for the program in the Tigre province in northern Ethiopia, thus doubling the territory assigned to the ALC missionaries.

Because of the excellent work done by the Swedish and other European Lutheran missionaries, there were already 30,000 Lutherans in

Ethiopia when the ALC missionaries arrived. In retrospect, one of the Ethiopian church leaders expressed the opinion that one of the most important contributions of the American Lutheran missionaries was their insistence that all missions join together with the Ethiopian Lutherans and form a single Lutheran church. The time was ripe and the Americans acted as a catalyst to bring the other Lutheran missions together. Indeed, other Lutheran missionaries had frequently talked about this possibility, but for various reasons, had never seriously proceeded with the plans. Missionary Schaefer himself was a strong believer in having one Lutheran church in Ethiopia that would include all the work done by the various missions. This one Lutheran church should have the authority to write its own constitution and should also have authority over the missionaries assigned to Ethiopia by Lutheran churches or mission societies. In 1959 the Ethiopian Evangelical Church—Mekane Yesus, was organized.

The first five years of the ALC mission in Ethiopia were difficult. Pioneer challenges always attract people with strong wills. That's what makes them pioneers. But when strong wills get together there is also misunderstanding. These misunderstandings resulted in a rapid turnover of missionary personnel during the first several years of ALC activity in Ethiopia. Possibly another factor contributing to the turnover during the first decade was the culture gap between Americans and Ethiopians.

Mekane Yesus was, after all, an Ethiopian church—in fact and not just in name—and Ethiopians exercised their full authority. It's not difficult to see that misunderstanding could easily develop between them and Americans who had different standards of organizational efficiency and independence.

One of the factors that has given strength to the Lutheran Church in Ethiopia during these years is the strong Mekane Yesus congregation that was formed in Addis Ababa during the Italian occupation when Lutherans came down from Eritrea and settled in the capital. This congregation actually was the representative before the government in behalf of all the Lutherans, and through their leadership they could approach the emperor and get permission for programs that other evangelical missions found hard to get. One reason the Lutherans were so successful is that they had capable spokesmen before the government.

Some of the more progressive people of the country belong to the Mekane Yesus Church. For 35 years the Ethiopian ambassadors to London have been Lutherans. There have never been less than six ambassadors in various Ethiopian embassies all over the world who have been members of the Mekane Yesus Church. A number of its members hold top positions in the army and police and some of them are cabinet ministers.

Very few of the old nobility belong to the Mekane Yesus Church. There is a silent tension between the progressive people who have risen to top positions in the country and those who are influential because they belong to the old families and may not be that interested in the improvement of life for the common man.

Today the Mekane Yesus Church is composed of five synods, each with a high degree of independence. The North Ethiopia Synod is the area where the ALC missionaries are at work. It includes the southern part of Addis Ababa itself and the Wollo, Tigre, and Begemdir provinces to the north. The Central Synod includes the area where the Swedish Evangelical Mission has been active. The Western Synod is the largest of the five synods and includes the churches started by German and Swedish missionaries. The South Ethiopia Synod is comprised of the churches started by Norwegian and Danish missionaries. The Kambatta Synod came to Mekane Yesus from the outside. It represents churches that had been started by one branch of the Sudan Interior Mission who felt great kinship with the Lutherans and asked to become a part of Mekane Yesus.

Membership statistics for these five synods for 1970 were as follows:

Synod	Churches	Pastors	Baptized Members
Central	68	9	6,275
South	768	27	43,364
Western	206	29	71,559
North	34	9	2,611
Kambatta	127	19	19,108
Total	1,203	93	142,917

6

relationship of the alc to the north ethiopia synod

Our comments at the beginning of this book indicated that this would not be a comprehensive account of all five synods of the Evangelical Church—Mekane Yesus. Since the book is intended particularly for the members of the American Lutheran Church, special attention will be given to the smallest of the five synods, the North Ethiopia Synod, because that's where ALC missionaries are stationed. This chapter, therefore, is a brief overview of facts, figures, and institutions in which members of the American Lutheran Church have greatest interest.

The North Ethiopia Synod has 2,611 baptized members, 34 congregations, and 9 pastors. Ato Berhe Beyene, a layman, is the full-time executive secretary. After two years of college in Ethiopia he came to California Lutheran College, where after two years he earned his BA degree as well as a master's degree in business administration and human relations at Pepperdine College in Los Angeles.

Each of the 34 congregations is allowed to send one delegate to the annual convention of the synod. Every two years delegates from the churches of all the synods are elected to a convention of the national church body, the Evangelical Church—Mekane Yesus.

The North Ethiopia Synod has a current annual budget of about $220,000 (American dollars). Of this amount, $160,000 is the contribution of the American Lutheran Church, and $60,000 comes from the Ethiopians. Of this $60,000, $10,000 comes from offerings within the congregations and the remaining $50,000 comes from such sources as fees at the hospitals, schools, and sale of farm products.

In addition the ALC also pays the salaries of the missionaries who work in the North Ethiopia Synod. The synod has a ten-year plan, through which it hopes to bring its congregations to the point that they will be able to carry all of the expenses of their evangelistic work. Subsidy from the United States will still be necessary to support some of the institutions such as the hospital, the agricultural schools, the seminary, and the literature program. While the missionaries receive their salary from the ALC, they are placed by, work under, and are responsible to the North Ethiopia Synod. (The synod is composed mostly of Ethiopians, although the missionaries themselves and the International Lutheran Congregation, a multi-racial congregation in Addis Ababa, are also members of the synod.)

ALC missionaries are stationed in three general areas: in Addis Ababa (population of about 800,-000), the capital of Ethiopia; in the Wollo Province in the towns of Dessie (about 60,000 people), Wuchalle, and Waldia, about 375 miles northeast of Addis, and in the Axum, Selek-leka, Adua area, about 400 miles north of Dessie.

In Addis Ababa itself the office and the home of the executive secretary of the North Ethiopia Synod, the Mekane Yesus Seminary, one of the studios for Radio Voice of the Gospel, and the homes of several missionaries are located in one general area. One of the missionaries living here is also pastor of the International Lutheran Church, which has services in both English and Amharic. Another is the director of the seminary. Since the seminary serves not only the North Ethiopia Synod but some of the other synods of Mekane Yesus as well, missionaries from other countries who teach at the seminary also live here.

In another part of the city is the national office of the Mekane Yesus Church, and in still another part of the city is the transmitting studio of the Radio Voice of the Gospel. There are also several congregations in Addis Ababa, and from time to time a missionary serves as full-time pastor of an Ethiopian congregation, functioning much the same way as a pastor of a congregation in America would carry on his duties.

Good Shepherd School, also in Addis Ababa, is not an official part of the mission or the church, but is a separate corporation of a number of Protestant missions in Ethiopia, which provides an American education for the children of missionaries.

About 25 miles outside of Addis is Debre Zeit, where a boarding high school and teacher training college is operated jointly by Mekane Yesus and some of the Lutheran synods. An ALC missionary is a member of the faculty here. The high school has an above average record in the number of graduates that pass government examinations for admission into the universities.

The chief task of the ordained missionaries in the Dessie-Wuchalle-Waldia area is to assist Ethiopian pastors and evangelists serving the congregations in this area. The plight of most pastors and evangelists is that they have very few books and little or no opportunity for spiritual refreshment at conferences or programs of continuing education. Missionaries conduct Bible studies with them and in general try to encourage them and help them in their work. Since there are not enough Ethiopian pastors for all the congregations, the missionaries rotate among the churches and usually conduct services somewhere every Sunday. This may mean traveling by land rover or riding for an hour and a half or more by mule.

There is also an agricultural school at Tisa Abalima near Wuchalle where ten selected Ethiopian families live for a year to learn improved methods of agriculture. Each family is given a plot of ground while in school and they get to keep all the grain they can grow. An American agriculturalist has been the director of this school, but an Ethiopian is currently studying in the United States with the understanding that he will become the director.

In addition to a congregation in Dessie, served by an Ethiopian pastor, there is also a hostel for boarding students who go to the government school. The hostel is operated by the synod, with an Ethiopian in charge of the program. After school hours he conducts informal classes in religion and provides opportunities for fellowship for the students. The operation of hostels is becoming an increasingly popular and effective way for the church to reach the student population. The operating costs are low, for the students pay for their own room and board.

The mission built a hospital at Waldia, but difficulty in getting doctors has kept the program curtailed. There are several missionary nurses at Waldia as well as an ordained missionary who works with the local pastors and evangelists in the area.

The whole Dessie area is a stronghold for Muslims. Quick progress was made in winning these people for the Christian faith in the last few years, but the program has slowed considerably, and many of those who did become Christians have not remained active in the church. Nevertheless, there is a cautious optimism that there will be long-range slow and steady growth. There are also a number of literacy schools in this area. Missionaries play an enabling role in the supervision of these schools.

An interesting development is taking place in the Tigre Province in the area of Axum, Selek-Leka, and Adua. One of the objectives of the Mekane Yesus Church is, whenever possible, to help strengthen and renew the Ethiopian Orthodox Church. In the Selek-Leka area there is an unusually warm relationship between the ALC ordained missionary and the Orthodox priests. The ALC missionary is asked to speak in Orthodox churches virtually every Sunday, and feels that he is serving in a better way by helping to renew that church than by trying to get fallen away Orthodox to join a Lutheran church.

There is also an agricultural school in Selek-Leka with the same purpose as the school in Wuchalle. In addition, the lay missionary, who is the director of this school has helped the farmers form a cooperative so that they learn something about the skills of marketing. A hospital that was started here had difficulty getting missionary doctors, so it has been turned into a health station and clinic, with an Ethiopian health officer in charge. One section of the former hospital is being used for grain storage by the cooperative, so that grain can be held for sale when the market price is favorable.

One ALC missionary is stationed at the teacher training institution at Adua. This school has achieved quite a reputation for helping to train many of the leaders of the church in various parts of the country.

One of the problems that quickly becomes obvious to one who visits the country is that the economy makes it impossible for the church itself to support expensive institutions such as hospitals, agricultural schools, and teacher training schools. Were we to start from scratch again, it is doubtful that we would invest huge sums of money in institutions. Little is gained by debating whether we should or should not have started institutions when we did. Times have changed. Since governments are also building hospitals, it is now unwise for missions to duplicate the government's efforts. The consensus of missionaries in Ethiopia is that the success of the medical program there has been something less than glorious.

Maybe it can be resurrected, but certainly not at the expense and on the budget of the Ethiopian church. The Ethiopian church is fully determined to become financially independent in its evangelistic program and the growth of its congregations. For the present at least if the institutions are to be maintained, the funds will have to come from churches and mission societies outside the country. The lesson for the future seems to be to encourage governments to build such institutions as schools and hospitals and let the church supply men with dedication to serve in them. In some instances the government itself will pay the salaries of the medical missionaries, thus freeing mission dollars to be devoted to evangelistic work.

There is no question about a great need for more medical and educational institutions, and church and government are both short of funds to maintain them. Perhaps the solution lies in a massive coalition of church, government, and international agencies.

Ethiopia is divided into 14 provinces. Most of the work of the North Ethiopia Synod of the Mekane Yesus Church, that synod with which missionaries from the American Lutheran Church are most closely affiliated, is centered in Tigre and Wollo provinces. A few North Ethiopia Synod churches are also located in Addis Ababa in the Shoa province and in Gondar in the Begemdir Province. The northernmost province, Eritrea, is now a part of Ethiopia. It became the means by which Italy entered the affairs of Ethiopia in the late 19th century and in the 1930's (see Chapter 3).

The church at Robit described in Chapter 8.

The custom of chatting after church is universal. Members of the Mekane Yesus congregation in Addis Ababa gather in front of their church after services.

Dr. Herbert Schaefer (center), first ALC missionary to Ethiopia, is shown in an audience with His Majesty Emperor Haile Selassie.

Africa Hall in downtown Addis Ababa, the headquarters for the Organization of African Unity.

Four leading members of the Evangelical Church — Mekane Yesus. Left to right: Baissa Jammo, vice president; Emmanuel Abraham, president; Kes Badema Yalew, a retired pastor; and Ato Gebre-Ab, an active layman.

Threshing in many places in Ethiopia is still done as it was in Old Testament times. Oxen tread out the grain, which is then thrown into the air for wind to blow the chaff away.

An orthodox church in Axum.

A Coptic priest in Ethiopia displays his ancient illustrated Bible. The parchment manuscript is more than 300 years old.

His Imperial Majesty, Haile Selassie, arrives for the inauguration of the Lutheran World Federation Broadcasting Station (Radio Voice of the Gospel), Addis Ababa.

An engineer at the Radio Voice of the Gospel transmitting station.

7

new experiments in education

Traditionally, when western churches have sent missionaries to Africa or Asia, a high priority in their program has been the establishment of a seminary. This has seemed logical, for the church has always felt its main task is to preach the gospel. So, why not develop seminaries to train preachers? Naturally, missionaries had to be the first professors until such a time as nationals themselves had been brought to the level that they could teach. This meant that the curriculum itself was designed by westerners and usually after a western pattern. There were adaptations, of course, to fit local needs, but they were just that—adaptations—which implied that the western pattern was still the norm. There seemed to be no such thing as starting from scratch with the original thought patterns of the nationals. As nationals themselves became competent they assumed prominent roles, but by that time their own understanding of the gospel had been filtered through the mind of a western theologian. Today, however, nationals are becoming more and more astute in developing a theology that springs out of their own soil instead of being transplanted.

Now the question is becoming more radical: Do we really need the kind of seminary at all where students are cloistered for several years for intensive study and then sent back to the bush or the metropolis to be ministers? Even more radical: Can we really go on the assumption that the full-time, ordained, paid clergy is always the ideal, and anything else only second best until the ideal can be achieved?

Mekane Yesus is beginning to ask these questions. Their first answer was the traditional one: build a seminary. Hardly had the American Lutheran Church sent missionaries to Ethiopia when it already supplied funds for a seminary. Some of the brighter men with good potential—particularly those who had a good background in the teacher training institute of the Swedish Lutheran mission—were chosen as students for the seminary and given full scholarships. Other missions sent a few students, so the seminary became a joint operation of the Synods and Mekane Yesus. Small though the student body was, it provided hope for a trained, full-time clergy.

But the church has been having some second thoughts. The poverty of the people being what it is, will they ever be able to pay full-time clergy? And can a church really exist as an independent church if it is destined for long generations to be dependent on foreign subsidy to pay its clergy? The other factor that caused some rethinking was the experience of some of the students who went to a congregation after spending several years in the seminary.

Since most of the congregations are in the villages and the seminary is in Addis Ababa, the seminarians are far removed from the kind of life they will be called to minister to when they graduate. Instead of being equipped to serve these people, the gulf between them and their people is often widened while they are in the seminary.

An extension seminary was devised to help solve this problem. This kind of seminary was pioneered in Latin America. It goes on the assumption that the full-time paid ministry may not necessarily fit the situation in every country. Perhaps Ethiopia is one of those places that should be more dependent on worker-priests and tent-making ministries. The extension seminary takes the seminary to the students instead of bringing the students to the seminary.

Missionary Loren Bliese, who is the director of both the seminary in Addis Ababa and the extension seminary, goes into the provinces for a few days every month to conduct a training program for men who will continue their regular occupation but will also become a leader and a pastor in a local congregation. Other missionaries in the area follow up on the assignments given by Missionary Bliese and assist the student-workers as much as they can between the visits of Pastor Bliese.

National church leaders in Ethiopia point out that a wide variety of pastors and church leaders are needed. Pastors in village congregations where most of the members are still illiterate will probably not find the seminary in Addis Ababa the best place for them to get theological training to meet their needs. On the other hand, a pastor for the large Mekane Yesus congregation in Addis Ababa, which includes many educated leaders in its membership, needs the kind of education given at Addis Ababa, with probably a year or two of theological study in Europe or America.

Furthermore, Mekane Yesus is also a part of world Christendom. It is a member of the Lutheran World Federation and the World Council of Churches. Consequently it must have some theologians and churchmen who are able to converse with church leaders of other countries.

Missionary Bliese's concept of seminary education is that it ought to be flexible enough to meet the needs of the church by providing theological education for candidates at differing levels of education. The European and American tradition of high academic attainments may not fit everywhere in Ethiopia at this time, and he believes we should adapt the system to the needs of the church. The extension seminary is able to tailor its programs to meet a variety of needs of the church.

In Ethiopia the church and the missions have

not been as heavily involved in primary and secondary education in recent years as they have in some countries of Africa and Asia. In earlier years the Swedish mission did start some schools, but particularly since the reign of Haile Selassie there has been heavy emphasis on government schools. Any graduate of a teacher training school can be assured a job in the government schools. Because there is still a great shortage of schools, Mekane Yesus operates a few elementary schools.

A high school and two teacher training schools are conducted within the North Ethiopia Synod— a high school and a teachers' college at Debre Zeit, referred to earlier in this book, and a teacher training institute at Adua, inherited from the work of the Swedish mission in northern Ethiopia. At present there are 33 students at Adua and 163 in the high school department at Debre Zeit, and 8 in the college department. The faculties include Ethiopians as well as missionaries from various churches cooperating with Mekane Yesus.

While many of the students at these schools are members of Mekane Yesus, there are also others who make no bones about the fact that they have questions about the validity of the church. Some of the graduates will teach in the few elementary schools still operated by the church, but many will teach in government schools.

We spent a delightful day at Debre Zeit and addressed several of the classes. There was no problem getting the high school students involved in discussion. They spoke openly about world problems, the place of Ethiopia in today's world, their opinion of the United States — which was generally, but not entirely, favorable — Christianity, and their own future.

It is in the schools of Ethiopia that one always finds the greatest hope and challenge. Here the future is at stake, and it should not be surprising that there are at times differences of opinion as to how a school should be run. There are some who feel that the school at Debre Zeit should put more emphasis on training for church leadership. They argue that students ought to be obligated in some way to serve the church, particularly since many of them are on full scholarship from the church. Others argue that if the gospel isn't powerful enough to put a claim on students, it is useless to demand of the students ahead of time that they commit themselves to the church. This school of thought holds that it's important to get more educated people in the Ethiopian society, and that the church is serving a useful function just to help educate the public. If the graduates then also become leaders in the church, fine. Church leaders hope this will happen, and they have a faculty that gives a good witness for the church, but there has been some disappointment that not more of the graduates have become active laymen in the church.

In recent years an increasing number of girls have enrolled in Debre Zeit. One of the problems of Ethiopia is the growing educational gap between husbands and wives. As more men are educated, there is greater difficulty in finding wives for them who will match their intellectual status.

Some church leaders would like to make Debre Zeit into an all girls boarding school, but this will probably not happen in the near future. Their argument is that boys already have a better opportunity for education, because the custom of the country allows for boys to live away from home in hostels or with relatives in larger towns and go to school there. It is still not customary for girls to live away from home and go to school unless it is a boarding school. There is a demand, therefore, for schools such as Debre Zeit, particularly for girls. An all girls boarding school is being started at Gondar under the auspices of the North Ethiopian Synod, with capital funds supplied by the Lutheran World Federation.

There is still a vast shortage of schools in Ethiopia. As recently as 1958 there were only 900 students that graduated from all the high schools of the country in that one year. Nine hundred high school graduates in one year out of a population of 22,000,000 is indeed a low figure. Our local high school in the United States, in a community of less than 50,000, graduates more than that in one year.

But these figures need to be seen in a larger perspective. The whole educational system of the country virtually had to be rebuilt after the Italian occupation. The emperor decided on a policy known as "a narrow shaft instead of a broad base." Instead of beginning with a broad base of education for all in the elementary years and then adding secondary and college levels after the primary children are brought to that level, the emperor decided on a "narrow shaft" of education at all levels. A considerable number of college graduates were produced quickly, and progress was made at all levels.

The need for schools is so great that even if the church would operate more schools, it still would not be competing with government schools. Church schools, however, are the exception rather than the rule, at least in the North Ethiopia Synod. The church is finding that its greatest contribution to education is to support the government schools.

The church does have an opportunity to provide a spiritual ministry by providing hostels in the larger cities where the schools are. After the capital investment of the building itself is provided, the operating cost is relatively small. Students who live here pay room and board. A full-time church staff person is in charge of the hostel and the program, which consists of formal Bible studies, informal discussions and social events.

One of the problems of the educational system in Ethiopia as well as in other African and Asian countries is that a disproportionately large number of graduates want to go into government service or the professions. For an educated person to be engaged in labor is a disgrace. Consequently few men of leadership ability go into engineering or trades or business to give leadership to the upbuilding of the economy of the country. One contribution the church is making is to emphasize a stewardship of life that instills pride in the upbuilding of the material side of the nation as a truly Christian virtue. But there is still room for more experiments in education.

8

trying to see ethiopia through ethiopian eyes

Trying to understand and interpret the work of the church in a different culture involves three steps. First, there is simply the matter of observing personally what is happening around you. This we tried to do by spending several weeks in Ethiopia, talking and living with missionaries and the leaders and members of the Ethiopian church and as much as possible immersing ourselves in their lives.

Second, there is the recognition that since we are Americans, the way we understand what we see will be colored by our own background. We need, therefore, to try to see Ethiopia through Ethiopian eyes, to think ourselves "into the skin of the Ethiopians," so that as much as possible we can feel as they feel. To really understand a culture one has to make a determined effort to see things from the point of view of those in that culture instead of comparing them with our culture.

Third, we now need to get back out of the skin of the Ethiopian and get into the skin of the people to whom we want to communicate and translate what we learned into language meaningful to their experiences.

One of our problems as middle-class affluent Americans is that we attach value judgments to economic status. We don't intend to do this, but we are so much a part of an affluent culture that even when we know better we still subconsciously feel that people who are poor are less capable — if not less moral — than those who are middle class.

Because we have a compulsion for cleanliness — some people actually think that "cleanliness is next to godliness" is a quotation from the Bible— we automatically pass a value judgment on people who feel no guilt about tattle-tale gray or blotchy shirts. Because comfort and affluence are so much a part of our everyday life, we find it difficult to imagine that people can exist meaningfully in extreme poverty.

A missionary who knows the language and people of Ethiopia well said that he lived quite closely with the people and was always amazed at how happy they could be. Their extreme poverty builds interdependence and community. People help one another in times of trouble. Affluence, as in the United States, has a tendency to bring individualism and isolation, if not selfishness, and destroy the sense of community. In the late afternoon and early evening when their day's work is done, the Ethiopians are likely to gather in the village or the neighborhood for an hour or two just to talk.

"They wouldn't trade this community for our isolation," the missionary said. "They are really very stoical about suffering. We read a lot of suffering into their lives that may not be there except from our perspective."

There is no sense in trying to minimize the problem of their poverty or excuse ourselves from doing something about it, or in any way trying to make believe that they like it that way. After all, hunger is painful for them too. Nor are we trying to make a case for a romantic acceptance of poverty. We simply point out that it is a given of life for many Ethiopians.

Although the abundant life that the gospel holds out also includes the hope of freedom from hunger and suffering, the gospel must also be meaningful to them while they are in poverty. The realistic facts of life are that they will probably stay there for a long time.

It's difficult to even put it into concrete terms. To say that the average Ethiopian has an annual income of $55 is true, but it doesn't really help us very much in understanding the situation. Somehow or other these people still live as we probably would too if the situation were that desperate in our country, but our whole style of life would be changed. How could the gospel be made meaningful in that different style of life?

It was a common sight to see 85-pound women

each carrying a hundred-pound clay water pot full of water or a 125-pound bundle of eucalyptus branches on her back. Most of the people in the rural areas live in a one-room house, in which the whole family sleeps, eats, cooks, and lives — at times sharing it with a few animals.

Nor should we suppose that once Ethiopians begin to develop a higher standard of living that then they automatically start thinking like Americans. Even among the more affluent Ethiopians marriages for their children are still largely arranged by the parents. While we Americans may think this is a hopelessly outmoded system — and in the urban areas of Ethiopia, arranged marriages are giving way to the free choice of the couple — one very highly educated Ethiopian expressed regret that some of the advantages of family-arranged marriages are being overlooked. He argued for a modified system in which the wishes of the bride and groom are taken into account but in which some of the strengths of the old system are kept.

In family-arranged marriages, the two families are usually good friends who have known each other for many years. The bride and groom have the support of both families, who will give them assistance in helping make a marriage work when there are difficulties. The bride has two persons outside of the family who act as guarantors. Anytime she has a problem with her husband she can go and stay with her guarantors for a week. They go to the husband and try to understand the problem and work for a reconciliation before the wife's parents are approached.

While divorce is on the increase in Ethiopia as it is in all countries, it is much more prevalent in the case of husbands and wives who have freely chosen each other than among those whose parents participated in the arrangement. Even in America there are sociologists who point to the weakness of the "nuclear" family which includes just the husband and wife and their children. A strong case is made for the "extended" family, which includes grandparents and relatives. Maybe the Ethiopians can teach us that marriage is fundamentally much more of a larger family affair than just the two people getting married.

Ethiopians have a high respect for authority. The Amharic language provides many forms for flattery, adulation, and expressions of deference toward those in authority. A leader loses status if he shares his authority with someone under him. This characteristic has advantages as well as disadvantages. One of the advantages is that once an authority figure is willing to bring about change, it will usually come. One of the disadvantages is that it is difficult to express honest differences of opinion. It is difficult, therefore, for a junior government officer to suggest improvements in the system without being suspected of disloyalty.

One characteristic of the Ethiopians that causes a problem for the development of leadership in the church is the extreme respect for elders. On the one hand, young leadership is developing in the church; but on the other hand, because these leaders are young they have a difficult time being acknowledged for their ability.

Americans trying to evaluate the contributions of missionaries to the church in Ethiopia have their own problems in trying to adapt their traditional standards of measuring to fit a life style that is totally different. An illustration of this is our own experience when we rode a mule for an hour and a half to go to church at Robit, a little village in the foot of the mountains near Wuchalle in the Wollo province.

We had been told that this area around Wuchalle had "opened up for the gospel" in an unusual way in the last few years. This success was looked upon as a real breakthrough, for this was the area in which the Muslims lived, and preaching the gospel had been notoriously difficult and unsuccessful among the Muslims. But now seemingly the secret of success had been found.

When we got to the church at Robit after our mule ride, services had already begun. There were eight people in church besides ourselves — the evangelist, who conducted the worship, five men, a woman with a small child, and a man standing outside the window looking in.

Any kind of romantic image I may have had about the glamour of mission work went quickly out that window. And as we rode our mules back to the missionary's home we were depressed and did a lot of thinking. Was this the way the church's mission dollars were being spent? At the moment we weren't too sure the program was worth supporting.

Had we been asked that evening to give a "strong pitch" for world missions at some church in the United States, we would have had a difficult time making our interest sound authentic. But then had we lived in the year 33 A.D. we might have had an equally hard time getting enthusiastic about the possibility of 12 men — most of them unsophisticated fishermen — being equal to the task of taking the gospel into all the world.

Before we could understand the story of Robit and its seeming lack of success, we had to think through the kind of background from which we came and against which we were trying to measure success.

We are Americans, middle-aged, and Lutherans of conservative background. Since many of the readers will very likely fall into one or more of these categories, their first impressions of the Robit experience would probably have been similar to ours. We grew up at a time when foreign missions — as it was known then — seemed to be the most exciting part of the church's work. Mission festival Sunday was a big event of the church year. It was usually an all-day affair with two mission sermons in the morning and two in the afternoon and a picnic lunch at noon.

Whenever possible the pastor arranged for a missionary on furlough to be the guest speaker. It was always a thrill to hear the success stories of missionaries. It was impressive to hear of the impact that the gospel made on the lives of people in primitive — according to our standards — cultures. Before the gospel came, many of them were cannibals. After the gospel came, they threw away their instruments of war and magic and large numbers of them were baptized.

We're not suggesting that the missionaries exaggerated. It's simply a fact that in the brief time of one sermon there is only so much a missionary can do. The message that came through was that the mission program was highly successful in terms of numbers "won for the kingdom," and that this program merited our prayers and financial support because there were still many who had not heard the gospel.

A favorite mission hymn said it this way:

Behold, how many thousands still are lying
Bound in the darksome prison house of sin,
With none to tell them of the Savior's dying,
Or of the life He died for them to win.

Another stanza in that same hymn plainly suggested that money given to missions was a good investment:

Give of thy sons to bear the message glorious;
Give of thy wealth to speed them on their way;
Pour out thy soul for them in prayer victorious;
And all thou spendest, Jesus will repay.

83

We are production and success oriented. We like to measure and count, and it's by counting that we measure the success of enterprises. Had there been 200 people in church at Robit that Sunday we would have pronounced the work of the church a success, but that opinion might have been just as superficial as calling it a failure because there were only eight in church. The criteria to judge the effectiveness of the mission of the church are far more complex than counting people at a worship service.

So now let's begin again with that Sunday in Robit when there were eight persons in church. We were told that a year ago there had been over 100. What had happened? To be perfectly fair, we should report that this was in the middle of the harvest season and many of the people who otherwise might have been in church felt they had to work in the harvest. But quite apart from that understandable reason, the fact was that there had been a great drop in interest. Why?

The missionaries had tried an experiment here a few years ago. For a while it seemed to be successful, but it is now generally conceded to have left some bad after-effects. The experiment was to give a small amount of money to people so they could buy food during a six-week period of intensive adult instruction. The missionary understood quite well that it was a hazardous experiment, but thought it worth the attempt.

The danger was that it would be interpreted as paying people to become Christians. On the positive side, it was argued that these people were so poor that they simply couldn't afford to be away from their fields. They just plainly needed food. Furthermore, the practice is not totally unlike a custom in the churches in the United States that pays food, travel, and lodging to people brought together for some church conferences.

For years we have given scholarships to students who have shown promise, so that they could become pastors. Where then does one draw the line and decide that after this point in a Christian's development it is acceptable to pay for his education but before this point it is wrong? Why should it be less holy to pay a person 35 cents a day for food for a six-month period than to pay a seminary student $30 or more a month for four years?

In theory the argument sounds reasonable; in practice the idea ran into some problems. The hope was that if they were paid this small amount as a food allowance for a short period of time they would quickly gain the spiritual depth that would make this kind of monetary encouragement unnecessary. What happened, however, was that many of them came to instruction as long as they were being paid and then stopped coming. Some of the people who came later came in the hope of being paid and complained that they weren't being treated as the earlier converts had been treated.

The fact was, however, that there were a

number who did come and who did hear the gospel for the first time and who were converted. While there may indeed have been some who fell away when the pay stopped, at least a beach-head was gained in the center of Muslim terri-tory. Whether the method that was used was right or wrong is immaterial now. The Mekane Yesus Church has rejected this method as a pro-gram for evangelism. There *were* eight people in church in Robit that Sunday in December. Maybe this will be a nucleus on which to build. Without this experiment — hazardous as it now may seem in retrospect and was understood to be such by the missionary even then—there might have been none.

Eleven congregations have now been formed in a twenty-mile area in the Wollo province in which Robit is located, giving an evangelical witness in the villages that are largely Muslim. Five congregations were started in adjacent areas after the courses were stopped for which people were given food allowances. A Bible school in the nearby town of Worgessa has resulted in the baptism of Muslim priests. Not only are these priests brought to Christianity, but they often become literacy teachers and part time evange-lists.

There are areas where the Mekane Yesus Church has been successful numerically, even according to American standards. For instance, this church is the fastest growing Lutheran church in Africa, if not in the world. It has been averaging a growth of 15 percent a year. Indeed, in 1970 it grew by 27 percent. But a growth like this poses different problems in Ethiopia than it would in the United States.

If the American Lutheran Church, with a confirmed membership of about 1,750,000 were suddenly to grow 15 percent in one year, that would mean 262,500 members. Since the ALC has about 4,800 congregations, this would average about 55 new members per congregation. Furthermore, since most of these new members would probably have gone through an instruction period of from two to eight weeks and would already have had some acquaintance with the church before, they could come in and immediately begin to work.

But the growth of the church in Ethiopia does not spread out equally among all the congregations like that. It comes largely in whole new areas where there are no existing congregations to absorb the new members. It would be more like if the American Lutheran Church would add a whole new geographic district each year where there had been few ALC churches before. This district would need support from the rest of the church until it got established.

But even this would not be a major problem in the United States. We are people of affluence and education. We know how to arrange financing and mortgages over a long period of time. And even though the new members might have come from non-Lutheran or even non-Christian backgrounds they at least would not have been totally ignorant of what the church is all about.

Things just aren't like that in Ethiopia. Not only are most of the Ethiopians who join the church so poor that they can contribute very little if anything, but in all likelihood they can't even read or write. When it is said, therefore, that the church increased by 27 percent in one year, that does not mean that all of these people come with a full understanding and ability to make a strong positive contribution to the church. According to our traditional way of looking at things, the chances are that for a few years they will be a "drain" on the resources and leadership of the church rather than a strength to help the church move forward. But again, this is only if we try to impose our own understanding of leadership on a situation that is totally different.

It is not improbable that conditions in Ethiopia are similar to the account of the first Pentecost as described in Acts. We are told that 3,000 were added to the church that day. It is quite possible that many of those 3,000 were more like Ethiopians who come to faith and are baptized than they are like adult Americans who already know something about Christianity and come into church membership after several weeks or months of instruction.

To understand the church in Ethiopia, therefore, one needs to try to understand it from the viewpoint of the Ethiopians themselves.

9

politics and land reform

There was a time when it was considered unwise to mix religion and politics. Some people
are still not comfortable with the idea. The fact
is it usually is not comfortable, least of all in
Ethiopia, but it is inescapable. It has always been
difficult for Lutheran missionaries in any country
to take an openly critical attitude toward the government. Even if they had strong critical attitudes
toward the government, they couldn't express
them, for if they did, they would be deported.
The whole Lutheran tradition is that government
is a gift of God. In this sinful, human society,
government may often be bad, but bad government is better than anarchy and revolution. The
position of the Lutheran Church has always been
to obey the government in power, and if it is
bad, to do everything possible to improve it.
Open revolution has never been advocated.

We cannot close our eyes to the fact that there
are those in Ethiopia who feel that the govern-

ment is repressive; just as there are those in America who feel the American government is repressive. Americans have greater freedom to say so than do Ethiopians. The accusation raises two questions: What other alternatives are there? What, if anything, can be done about it? There is a third question: Ought the church do anything, and if so, what?

In Ethiopia, as elsewhere, there is a difference of opinion between the young and the old. Young people quickly get impetuous. They see all the bad things. They want change. They haven't lived long enough to know what the alternatives are to the present system. Never having lived through a revolution they don't know what it can mean. Older people may also be aware of present inequities, but they can remember days that were much worse. In comparison, the situation of today seems quite bearable. For them the present is better than the past. They are hopeful about the future.

The facts of life are that the Emperor is almost 80 years old. He won't live forever. According to the constitution, the Crown Prince will succeed his father as Emperor. The big question is whether a succession of power can come without a revolution.

One student of the Ethiopian scene stated the problem this way: "The dilemma of the increasing number of modern educated Ethiopians is precisely this: although they can no longer accept the role of the Solomonic tradition and the concept of being 'chosen people' as the basis of the state, any more than they can accept that the Ethiopian Christian Church is fit to be the cement of their society, they are uncertain how to effect a change."

An attempt was made to overthrow the Emperor in 1960. Architects of the attempted *coup* were Germame Neway, who had been educated in the United States, and his brother, Mengistu Neway, who was in charge of the Imperial Guard. When the *coup* came to naught, Germame shot himself, and his dead body was hanged in public view. Mengistu was captured, tried, and executed.

In replying to his sentence of death Mengistu said, "Truly, because some people have died on my account, I feel a certain sorrow, but had God been willing a *coup* would have come about sooner or later. I did all this for the sake of the Ethiopian people and I pray that God soon gives true judgment to the Ethiopian people."

An underground group managed to arrange that he be abducted from his place of detention, but he refused to be freed. He undoubtedly believed his dead brother's oft-repeated remarks that, successful or not, their *coup* represented the vanguard of inevitable change. Mengistu said he preferred to die, and just prior to his execution, he said with great eloquence, "I go to tell the others the seed we set has taken root." Only time will tell whether the new myth growing around the Neway brothers and their attempted *coup d'etat* can ever quite displace the story of

Solomon and Sheba as an inspiration for the Ethiopian nation.

Germame was very critical of the church, but he also underestimated the influence that the church still had on the lives of the people. Some argue that the one reason the *coup* failed was that its leaders did not take into account the fact that the Ethiopian Orthodox Church had a strong hold on its people.

Today the Emperor is still in full control of the country. The Parliament is composed of two houses, the lower house, elected by the people, and the Senate, appointed by the Emperor. The Emperor has indicated on a number of occasions that eventually there must be a greater participation by the people, but he feels they are not ready for that yet.

Virtually everyone agrees that the number one priority to solve the problems of Ethiopia is land reform. Less than 200 families own most of the land of Ethiopia. The Emperor's family is said to own nearly 20 percent of all the land in the country. The Ethiopian Orthodox Church also has huge land holdings. Nearly every Parliament has had a land reform bill up for consideration, but so far none has passed. While we were in Ethiopia a bill was pending in Parliament that one person described as "having been watered down enough that I think this one might pass." But, he was quick to add, "it can't really be called a land reform bill; at most it's just one step, and there is a long, long way to go before we get what we really need."

The chief problem with the present land ownership system is that the owner decides every year what percentage of the crop he will take for rent. He always takes at least half. The plots that he rents out are always so small that the tenant can barely eke out a living. Furthermore, he has the right to expel the tenant from the land at will. Consequently, there is never an incentive for the farmer to improve the land or his methods of farming because he never knows how long he can stay on the land. The land reform bill under consideration at the present time calls for a fixed rent and the right of appeal of the tenant.

The landowner has a way of keeping the tenant in bondage to him. When the dry season starts and the farmer's supply of grain has run out, the landowner will sell back some grain to be repaid out of the next harvest.

Another one of the major problems of the country is the acceptance of bribes by government officials. Because of the constant economic stress under which most people constantly find themselves, income through bribes has become an accepted way of life. The Emperor's own reputation has never been tainted with the charge that he accepts bribes, and he tries desperately to improve the system, but the odds against improvement are staggering. The courts are always crowded with cases and it is assumed as a matter of course that some judges accept bribes.

An interesting development took place during the 1950s when Germame Neway was building his power base for the *coup*. He was given an appointment in a forsaken area in one of the provinces, and before long he built a school. When asked where he got the money to build the school, he publicly stated that he used money taken from bribes he had accepted. He said he disapproved very much of the practice of taking bribes, but since it was so much a custom, he felt that at least the money could be put to good use. This open admission did two things for Germame: It impressed the people with his honesty; and it brought in more money for the school, because those who had bribed him in the first place were now afraid that he would disclose where the bribes had come from, so they supported the school all the more.

There are, of course, exceptions to the accepting of bribes. Among the notable ones are some of the high officials in the government who are also leaders in the Mekane Yesus Church.

The church faces the serious question of how to act responsibly in a situation of this kind. Traditionally, it has kept free from all political entanglements, and for so doing it has earned itself the dubious reputation of condoning injustice. Mekane Yesus Church itself has done a good job of walking a middle road, recognizing that there may be many things wrong with the present government, but also recognizing that in the absence of a better alternative, the present government must be supported. It enjoys the confidence of the government and is able to minister to the people of Ethiopia as the country moves slowly toward a better economy and more democratic government. Whether the church can earn and keep the respect of the young intellectuals who feel the government is repressive, remains to be seen.

10

mekane yesus looks to the future

First impressions can be dangerously inaccurate. We could write many chapters describing depressing experiences in Ethiopia. The sight of crippled beggars and unbelievable poverty stays with you for a long time. But so does the sheer courage of men and women whose undaunted faith dares to believe that there is a future. At first you are almost afraid that any attempt to be optimistic is mere whistling in the dark. You are hopeful because you *want* to be hopeful, not because there is any substance to justify your hope. But maybe that's what the gospel is all about — as the writer to the Hebrews said (and it's worth reading it in five major translations):

"Now faith is the substance of things hoped for, the evidence of things not seen" — King James Version.

"Now faith is the assurance of things hoped for, the conviction of things not seen" — Revised Standard Version.

"Now faith means putting our full confidence

in the things we hope for; it means being certain of things we cannot see" — Phillips.

"And what is faith? Faith gives substance to your hopes, and makes us certain of realities we do not see" — New English Bible.

"To have faith is to be sure of the things we hope for, to be certain of the things we cannot see" — Good News for Modern Man.

The difficulty for Americans on a short visit is the impossibility of their getting over the culture shock of seeing outward conditions and never really getting acquainted with people enough to share in their everyday emotions of life — joy, sorrow, laughter, disappointment, pain, hope. We were impressed again — as we have been in other countries — with the marvelous spirit of missionaries. They have been able to enter into the daily experiences of the Ethiopians.

A story told us by one of the missionaries reminded us of the common humanity and emotions of all people. A husband had been forced to leave his wife and daughter because there was no job in the community. He went to find a job elsewhere and was not heard from for eight years. Friends of the wife urged her to forget him; he would never come back, they said. But she never doubted for a day that he would return. After eight years he did return, and they were reunited. The missionary tells the story of what happened after a year when another child was born. There was concern on the mother's face when she was told the baby was a girl. Every Ethiopian father wants a son. But the father was there, beaming smiles and said, "The girl's name will be 'Dink Nesh,' " which means, "You are wonderful." The look of happiness on the mother's face as a vindication of her faith was an inspiration to all of us, said the missionary. In fact, it was something of a parable of how hope is present in the midst of seeming futility.

As the church looks to the future it cannot help but be aware of its problems. The members of the church, after all, are human beings, and human beings are given to problems.

In the North Ethiopia Synod one of the major problems is tribalism. There are some historic origins for this problem. As pointed out earlier, the Lutheran Church in Ethiopia had its beginnings in Eritrea and the northern province of Tigre. Because the evangelical missions and opportunities for education came to these people earlier than they did to some of the rest of the people and country, they are more advanced and progressive. Consequently the Tigrinians have gotten more leadership positions in the North Ethiopia Synod. This is not true in the other synods nor in the officialdom of Mekane Yesus itself, where Gallas hold many important positions.

Annual conventions of the North Ethiopia Synod have sometimes become occasions for tribal jealousies and rivalries to come to the fore. While one may regret this, he should not be surprised about this turn of events. All he needs to do is to read the Book of Acts to find similar squabbles between the Greeks and the Jews. Or, he could read church papers in this country and find evidences of rivalries within Lutheran churches here. This is what the church is like, but God's strength has always been made perfect in such weakness.

Another problem related directly to the economic condition of the country is that the church easily attracts people to be paid evangelists and literacy teachers. While the salaries paid here are lower than they are for teachers in government schools and other government positions, these positions in the church are available to people with less education. Consequently, the danger is always present that people go into these positions in the church for the job opportunities rather than out of a deep sense of commitment or because of competence. But then, situations like that are not unknown in the United States either.

Despite these problems, one of the greatest assets of the Mekane Yesus Church is capable leadership that understands what the problems are and has the competence to do something about them. Reference has already been made to such men as Ato Berhe Beyene, the full-time executive secretary of the North Ethiopia Synod, and Ato Emanuel Abraham, a minister in the Emperor's cabinet, who is president of the Evangelical Church — Mekane Yesus. Other leaders include Ato Emanuel Gebre Selassie, an advisor at RVOG, who was the first president of Mekane Yesus; Pastor Gudina Tumsa, executive secretary of Mekane Yesus; Baissa Jammo, a member of the Senate, who is vice president of Mekane Yesus; Ato Hailu Wolde Semaiat, president of the large Mekane Yesus congregation in Addis Ababa and chairman of the Mekane Yesus Seminary Board, who is director of communications for the Ethiopian Airlines; and Ato Menkir Isaias, who earned a master's degree in the United States and is head of the public listening research department at RVOG. He is also one of the national officers of Mekane Yesus.

An example of evangelistic growth that has resulted from the presence of the American Lutheran Mission in Ethiopia is a congregation in Gondar. In 1965 Kes (Kes is the Ethiopian title for pastor) Tsehai Gebre Selassie, an Ethiopian pastor, had just returned to Ethiopia after a year at Luther Seminary in St. Paul. A man of deep conviction in his faith with an engaging personality, he was called by some evangelicals living in Gondar to begin a congregation. Today a beautiful new church, a parsonage and a soon-to-be-completed hostel for girls testify to the energy and resourcefulness of this man. The small group that called him as their pastor has now been joined by well over 100 additional believers.

Another major problem and challenge confronting the church of Ethiopia is how to become truly independent and develop its own life without relying too heavily on overseas financial support. Because of conditions of poverty, the temptation is always at hand to fall back on the financial support of affluent foreign churches, but the leaders of the Ethiopian church are resisting this temptation mightily. The temptation may be just as strong on the part of overseas mission boards to fund projects that they think are worthy without being fully cognizant of the feelings of the Ethiopians. That the Ethiopian church is making progress is evident, for instance, in the congregation that five years ago was getting $5,000 in subsidy and is now getting only $1,000. The hope is that all congregations will be self-supporting in ten years.

It is the dream of some of the missionaries that a new development within the church might be to have a social service program and to support and encourage social service programs being carried on by the government and other agencies. Some of this is already being done through community development agencies and such programs as the agriculture schools.

One program just developed by a group of Christians, in which members of Mekane Yesus played a leading role, is a telephone counseling service. A group of counselors are available to answer questions in the fields of marital problems, unemployment, and other matters of social concern. It is hoped that this service can be extended to include hospitals and other professional people so that the range of counseling can be broadened.

One non-church program that has attracted interest is the umbrella factory in Addis Ababa.

All employees of the factory are handicapped persons. One contribution of the church could be to give greater encouragement to more people and agencies to develop programs of this kind. The umbrella factory is adjacent to one of the Mekane Yesus churches. Some of the ladies of the International Lutheran Church are sponsoring a day nursery for the children of mothers who work in the factory. These are the kinds of social service projects, which if spurred on by the church, could do much to heal some of the social sores of the country.

A subject of continuous discussion and even some debate in Ethiopia as well as in the United States is the need for new missionaries. There are two schools of thought on this matter. One is that, heartless as it may seem, there is argument for withdrawing missionaries and literally forcing the young church to be more independent. This argument at least has some history in its favor — not only in Ethiopia, but in other countries as well. In New Guinea and Madagascar, for instance, when wars and persecutions have forced missionaries to leave the country, laymen carried on, and when the missionaries returned they were often amazed at the strength of the church. The same happened in Ethiopia during the Italian occupation, when Eritrean Lutherans moved down from Addis Ababa and kept the church intact until the missionaries returned. But why should we always be so surprised that God keeps his promise when he says that his word "shall not return to me empty, but it shall accomplish that which I purpose and prosper in the thing for which I sent it"?

One missionary points out that there is a difference, however, in missionaries being forced to leave and thus forcing the nationals to develop their own strengths, and in missionaries deciding of their own free will to leave and thus bringing discouragement to a church that feels it still needs assistance. Furthermore, there is the tremendous challenge and the opportunities facing the church in Ethiopia. We have reported that two hospitals in the Wollo and Tigre provinces had to cut back their services because of a lack of doctors. The nurse at one of these hospitals told us, "We had just gotten to the point that people were beginning to trust us. Instead of mothers waiting until they had complications in giving birth and coming to us only as a last resource — often when it was too late to do anything — they were now beginning to come a day or so before they expected to give birth to a child. This was a great victory for us. It showed that they were ready to trust us. And now we can't get a doctor."

There is no doubt that the need for missionaries is greater in all areas, ordained missionaries for evangelistic work as well as specialists in education, medicine, and other fields.

The question is probably not one of numbers but of relationships. How is it possible to meet all the needs and at the same time encourage the churches of Africa, Asia, and South America to develop an indigenous leadership that is truly indigenous and not a reflection of a western, affluent culture.

Probably no one is more aware of or more excited by the possibilities of how churches from various countries can work together than are the missionaries, mission executives, and mission boards. The field is open to imaginative new developments.

We who have so long felt that separation of church and state is almost a biblical doctrine are finding that there are some areas where they can work together to accomplish the will of God. If it is the will of God that hungry people be fed and that diseased bodies be given a chance for healing, and that curious minds be stimulated with education, then why can't church, industry, and government all work together, each contributing its own strengths.

The church's main task is to proclaim the gospel, but in that proclamation it must show concern for people. And one way to show concern is to imbue leaders of government and industry with the same kind of concern. In other words, if government and industry build schools and hospitals to educate and heal people, and farms and factories to provide food and clothing and shelter for people, then a contribution of the church is to provide men with insight and compassion to run schools, hospitals, industry, and governments.

11

translating interest
into involvement

Lack of involvement does not always mean a lack of interest. What is sometimes interpreted as a lack of interest in the world mission program of the church may rather be a lack of knowledge of how to express interest in action. Contrary to the opinion of many people, the financial contributions of churches throughout the country have increased during the last decade. The percentage of the offerings of congregations that has been sent to the national office of the denomination has not increased in proportion. In other words, people are giving more than they ever did before, but they are supporting different programs. It may not be a lack of interest that causes people to decrease their support of a certain program, it may be a lack of conviction that their support of a program really will make a difference.

The price of bigness is often lack of involvement. When a church body has nearly five thousand congregations and over two million members, it is difficult to feel that the contribution of one congregation or one member can be important. This feeling can be particularly prevalent when it comes to the world mission of the church. Even the work of the church can be complex and complicated at times. All of the work of the various boards is important — American missions, world missions, college education, theological education, youth, social service, evangelism. One is almost hesitant to list them for fear that an important one will be left out.

Is it possible for a person to be more interested in some than in others? And if he is, is it possible for him to contribute to special causes without being made to feel guilty because he is not equally interested in all programs? Is it even possible that the way God gets his work done is by interesting some people in some causes and others in other causes, or must we always insist that everybody at all times express an equal interest in all causes?

This is one of the great problems facing the church. The methods of supporting the work of the church have gone through cycles. There were times when there were so many causes seeking support within the church and congregations were bombarded with so many different appeals that a unified budget was adopted; all congregations and members were asked to contribute to a common treasury from which a variety of projects were funded.

That approach relieved the confusion of knowing which Sunday's offering to dedicate to which cause, but it removed people from personal involvement with a particular cause. And in time, lack of opportunity for involvement can lead to lack of interest.

If this book has led to a deeper interest in the world mission program of the church — and the work in Ethiopia in particular — how can that interest be translated into involvement? Involvement means at least three things:

1. *It has to do with people.* One of the reasons the program formerly known as "foreign missions" claimed such a high commitment from Christians was that it so readily involved people with other people. Missionaries were personally known in churches throughout the country. They were remembered personally in prayers by congregations and individuals. When they were home on furlough they criss-crossed the country, speaking in churches.

It was not uncommon for people to ask, "Do you have some special need? Is there a project we can support?" Through this kind of involvement as well as through their contributions to the general benevolence treasury of the church, many Christians throughout the country felt that they were participating personally in the world mission program of their church.

There is no reason to believe that opportunity for this kind of personal involvement has ceased or will cease. In fact, it is being encouraged. But one of the exciting things about today's mission enterprise is that the band of fellowship can be enlarged. Increasingly the role of the missionary is different today from what it was 50 years ago. More and more his role is to assist or enable the leaders of the church to which he has been sent. As we formerly were personally acquainted with and prayed by name for individual missionaries, so today we can get acquainted with churchmen from different countries.

In this book, for instance, you were introduced briefly to such men as Ato Berhe Beyene, Ato Emanuel Abraham, Ato Emanuel Gebre Selassie, Pastor Gudina Tumsa and others. These men have traveled in our country and have appeared in our churches. In the future more church leaders from other countries will visit our land. This increases the possibility of more personal involvement with more people.

This involvement whets our appetite for more information about and greater interest in countries where our missionaries are at work. We become more alert to newspaper and magazine articles about these countries. We no longer view political uprisings in other countries only on the basis of what may happen to our missionaries there, but we also develop a personal interest in the church there, its leaders and its members.

2. *Involvement means an awareness of a variety of structures through which the church can work.* A previous chapter raised the question of the relationship of the church and the mission to national governments. In earlier days when de-

mands for doctors and teachers were far greater than many of the economically underdeveloped countries could supply, the mission not only supplied doctors and teachers but also paid for building schools and hospitals. Later the governments often gave assistance in building these institutions and even helped pay salaries of teachers and doctors.

Whenever there is a change in procedure from one system and structure to another, there is usually a debate whether the change is an improvement or a retrogression. Equally intelligent people may have differing opinions, but there is general agreement among mission executives today that the variety of structures open to the church and to missionaries provides exciting challenges.

Because the demand for doctors and teachers is so great, the governments of some countries are willing to pay their salaries. This makes it possible for American churches to send more missionaries than their budgets would otherwise have allowed.

Furthermore, a person does not have to be directly connected with the mission to make a Christian witness. There is an increasing demand for personnel to fill positions in government and industry in other countries. American Christian laymen can take advantage of these opportunities, have an interesting position overseas, and at the same time join in the fellowship of the Christian church in those countries.

There are growing opportunities for overseas volunteer service programs. Through these programs doctors, dentists, nurses, carpenters, contractors, and business men in a variety of fields have given from three months to two years of their time in volunteer service in overseas countries and assisted the churches there. Congregations will find it interesting to get information on these opportunities by having missionaries or volunteer workers as speakers.

Nor should the traditional structure, the general benevolence program of the national church body be overlooked as probably still the most effective way of supporting the mission of the church in overseas countries. Support of special projects can be very intriguing and should be encouraged whenever possible, but it must be remembered that usually the only way special projects can be effective is if there is first a basic program undergirded by the general treasury of the church.

Two very effective ways in which individuals and congregations can become involved in a personal way in addition to the support of the general benevolence program of the church is through missionary sponsorships and scholarships. A congregation can decide to assume the salary of a missionary and thus have a closer personal touch with a particular missionary. Or, a congregation or an individual can assume the cost of sending a student in one of the overseas churches to school — either to a school in his own country or to a college or seminary in America or Europe.

Structures through which churches effectively carry out their programs change. Openness to new structures breathes new life into the church's mission task and makes possible deeper and more exciting involvement.

The day of missionaries is not over. The call today is not only for more missionaries but for a greater variety of missionaries—some short term, some long term, some ordained men, some laymen and lay women.

3. *Involvement means personal commitment to God.* There is a difference between the program of the church and the program of other institutions. We are not debating whether one is more important than the other. Very little purpose is served in carrying on such a debate. Nor are we saying that Christians should be concerned only about the program of the church or that they should downgrade the programs of other agencies. But we are saying that the church has a special kind of program and we at least need to be aware of what that program is and how it differs from other programs.

A person who is not a Christian or does not even believe in God can make a very valid contribution through the Peace Corps and other assistance programs of business and government, and it is not up to the Christian to pass judgment on people engaged in non-church programs.

But the Christian should recognize that the

church is a unique institution. From time to time it may cooperate with other institutions, but it must always remember its distinctive task. Its first obligation is a deep commitment to God and a desire to bear witness to the great truth that through Christ God has reconciled all people to him. The first task of the missionary must always be to proclaim that truth in word and deed.

Furthermore, the church has the promise of God that he will bless such efforts. It's no mere cliché, therefore, to urge Christians to pray for the mission of the church in our own land as well as overseas. And the prayer should be more than a perfunctory "God bless all the missionaries and the people to whom they minister."

Involvement in prayer means willingness to keep informed about the work of the church and to be used as a tool in the hands of God so that prayer can be answered. It means supporting liberally that for which you pray. The Bible says, "Where your treasure is there shall your heart be also." The converse of that is likewise true, "Where your heart is, there will your treasure be also." Interest in God's cause goes hand in hand with support of that cause through the structures that can carry out God's will.

In Ethiopia, one such structure is the Evangelical Church — Mekane Yesus. The close ties of Lutherans in Europe and America with fellow Christians in Mekane Yesus give added meaning to our confession of faith, "I believe in the Holy Ghost, the Holy Christian Church."